101 Easy Recipes

That You can Make with Less than 10 Minutes or Less!

By: <u>Emily Simmons</u>

Disclaimer:

The information presented in this book represents the views of the publisher as of the date of publication. The publisher reserves the rights to alter update their opinions based on new conditions. This report is for informational purposes only. The author and the publisher do not accept any responsibilities for any liabilities resulting from the use of this information. While every attempt has been made to verify the information provided here, the author and the publisher cannot assume any responsibility for errors, inaccuracies or omissions. Any similarities with people or facts are unintentional.

Table of contents

Table of contents 3
Introduction 7
Breakfast 8
    Multigrain Cereal 11
    Sausage Pepper Scramble 12
    Coconut and Raspberry Parfait 13
    Cinnamon French Toast 14
    Granola Yogurt Parfait 16
    Herbed Omelet 18
    Egg In A Hole 19
    Tomato Scrambled Eggs 21
    Sautéed Spinach and Poached Eggs 22
    Butter Eggs with Bacon and Spinach 23
    Smoked Salmon Creamy Eggs 24
    Potato Chip Frittata 25
    Zucchini Frittata 27
    Fresh Fruit with Yogurt Dip 28
    Sandwiches 29
    Cheddar Spread Sandwich 30
    Monte Cristo Sandwich 31
    Apple and Cheddar Sandwich 32
    Roasted Bell Peppers Sandwich 33
    Garlicky White Bean Sandwich 34
    Tuna Melt Panini 35
    Lemony Caper and Tuna Sandwich 36
    Cucumber and Avocado Sandwich 37
    Warm Fontina and Fig Sandwich 38

Salads 39
    Cold Potato Salad 40
    Spinach and Strawberry Balsamico Salad 41

- Plums and Mozzarella Salad 42
- Tomato and Basil Salad 43
- Watermelon and Blue Cheese Salad 45
- Citrus Fennel Salad 46
- Watercress Lemon Salad 47
- Caprese Salad 48
- Panzanella Salad 49
- Roast Beef Cabbage Salad 50
- Bell Pepper and Quinoa Salad 51
- Raw Zucchini and Sesame Salad 52
- Rice and Sweet Corn Salad 53
- Goat Cheese Salad 54

Main Dishes 56
- Garlic and Tomato Pasta 57
- Bok Choy Stir Fry with Peanuts 59
- Bacon and Avocado Scrambled Egg 60
- Sautéed Tilapia with Tomato Sauce 61
- Tomato Sauce Spaghetti 62
- Spicy Pecorino Spaghetti 64
- Lemon and Cilantro Roasted Salmon 65
- Shrimp and Spring Onion Stir Fry 66
- Pan Fried Sole 67
- White Wine Shrimps 68
- Quick Flatbread Pizza 70
- Quick Fried Rice 71
- Lettuce Wraps 73
- Chicken Wraps 74
- Cucumber and Yogurt Cold Soup 75
- Gazpacho 76
- Angel Hair Pasta with Smoked Trout 78
- Baked Eggs with Fresh Herbs 79
- Cajun Mushrooms 80
- Spinach and Cheddar Tortilla Melts 82
- Gooey Cheese Croissants 83

Cheese and Sausage Roll	84
Cheese Stuffed Mushrooms	85
Gnocchi with Three Cheese Sauce	87
Side Dishes	88
Spicy Snap Peas	89
Garlicky Sautéed Spinach with Sweet Corn	90
Yogurt and Blueberry Trifle	91
Crispy Couscous	92
Bacon Green Peas	93
Lemony Poached Asparagus	94
Chickpea Curry	95
Sautéed Tomatoes	96
Avocado and Tomato Salsa	97
Cheddar Grits	98
Caramelized Red Onions	99
Cheesy Creamed Corn	100
Cheese Cauliflower Sauté	102
Microwave Risotto	104
Dessert	106
Fruit and Mint Kebabs	107
Orange and Yogurt Salad	108
Yogurt and Blueberry Trifle	109
Microwave Chocolate Cake	111
Ricotta and Berry Dessert	112
Meringue and Strawberry Dessert	114
Melba Grilled Peaches	116
Yogurt with Pistachio and Strawberry Bowls	117
Grilled Pineapple and Ginger Sauce	120
Watermelon and Raspberry Salad	122
Banana Ice Cream	124
Beverages	125
Spinach Smoothie	128
Detox Juice	130
Chilled Fruit Shake	131

Margarita Shake 133
Conclusion 134

Introduction

We live in a world that is constantly changing, and we seem to be in a continuous rush. We rush to work, we rush back home, we rush when seeing our friends, we rush cooking. We are in a hurry at any moment of the day, and time seems to have compressed in the last few years. As a result we have bad eating habits, sleeping problems and stress, and we barely find ways to cope.

However, if you simply take a moment and look at things from the outside, you realize that they aren't that bad — it's all about perception and time management. We can fit it all in our schedule if we manage our time right and use little shortcuts — particularly in meal planning and preparation.

This cookbook offers you shortcuts for your morning meals, your main dishes, side dishes and desserts. They are all fail-proof recipes, delicious and easy to make, with ingredients that can easily be found in most supermarkets, if you don't have them in your pantry already.

All you have to do is find 10 spare minutes to create a dish that is nutritious and healthy, perfectly seasoned, and loaded with flavors.

So put that apron on and get cooking.

Breakfast

A rich and nutritious morning meal will give you enough energy to power through your morning. And it will also keep you away from unwanted snacks, thus helping you lose or maintain weight. With the following recipes, you have no excuse to skip breakfast.

1. Green Onion and Leek Omelet

Servings: 2-4

Ingredients:
6 eggs
1 leek, chopped
2 green onions, chopped
2 oz. feta cheese, crumbled
Salt, pepper to taste
3 tablespoons olive oil

Directions:
1. Beat the eggs with salt and pepper. Then stir in the leeks, green onions and feta cheese.
2. Heat the olive oil in a skillet and pour in the egg mixture.
3. Cook for a few minutes, flipping it over. Serve warm.

Multigrain Cereal

Servings: 2

Ingredients:
4 tablespoons quick cooking barley
4 tablespoons bulgur
4 tablespoons rolled oats
1 ½ cups almond milk
2 tablespoons raisins
1 pinch ground ginger
1 tablespoon brown sugar
1 banana, sliced
½ cup strawberries, sliced

Directions:
1. Combine the barley, bulgur, oats, almond milk, raisins, ginger and brown sugar in a saucepan.
2. Cook over medium heat for 5 minutes.
3. Remove from heat, spoon into serving bowls, and top with banana and strawberry slices before serving.

Sausage Pepper Scramble

Servings: 2

Ingredients:
2 tablespoons olive oil
2 chicken sausages, sliced
1 cup sliced mushrooms
1 red bell pepper, cored and diced
4 eggs, beaten
¼ cup grated Cheddar cheese

Directions:
2. Heat a skillet over medium heat and add the olive oil.
3. Place the sausages, mushrooms and bell peppers into the oil. Sauté for 5 minutes, then pour in the beaten eggs and cook 2-3 minutes, stirring all the time.
4. Remove from heat and add the grated cheese.
5. Serve right away.

Coconut and Raspberry Parfait

Servings: 4

Ingredients:
2 cups Greek style yogurt
2 tablespoons honey
1 mint leaf, chopped
½ cup shredded coconut
½ cup rolled oats
½ cup chopped almonds
2 cups fresh raspberries

Directions:
1. Mix the yogurt with the honey and mint in a bowl. In a different bowl, combine the coconut with the oats and almonds.
2. Layer the yogurt with the oat mixture and fresh raspberries in 4 serving bowls or glasses. Serve immediately.

Cinnamon French Toast

Servings: 2

Ingredients:
4 slices of sandwich bread
1 cup milk
2 eggs
½ teaspoon cinnamon powder
1 tablespoon honey
4 tablespoons butter

Directions:
1. Whissk the eggs with the milk, cinnamon and honey in a bowl.
2. Melt the butter in a skillet.
3. Dip each slice of bread into the milk mixture, then drop it into the hot butter.
4. Fry on both sides until golden brown.
5. Serve the toast warm, topped with your favorite jam.

Granola Yogurt Parfait

Servings: 4

Ingredients:
1 ½ cups granola
1 cup berries
1 ½ cups yogurt
2 tablespoons honey
1 teaspoon lemon zest

Directions:
1. Mix the yogurt with the honey and lemon zest.
2. Layer the yogurt with granola and berries in 4 serving bowls or glasses.
3. Serve right away.

Herbed Omelet

Servings: 2-4

Ingredients:
6 eggs
¼ cup heavy cream
2 tablespoons chopped parsley
2 tablespoons chopped dill
2 tablespoons chopped cilantro
1 teaspoon dried oregano
2 oz. mozzarella cheese, shredded
Salt, pepper to taste
4 tablespoons olive oil

Directions:
1. Beat the eggs in a bowl and stir in the heavy cream and aromatic herbs. Add salt and pepper to taste.
2. Heat the olive oil in a skillet.
3. Pour the egg mixture into the skillet and cook until golden brown on both sides.
4. When done, top with shredded mozzarella and serve.

Egg In A Hole

Servings: 2

Ingredients:
3 tablespoons olive oil
2 slices white or whole wheat sandwich bread
2 eggs
Salt, pepper to taste

Directions:

1. Heat the oil in a skillet.
2. Using a round cookie cutter, create a hole in the center of each bread slice.
3. Place the bread slices in the hot oil. Then crack open the eggs and drop them into the holes.
4. Season with salt and pepper and cook until the eggs are set.
5. Serve immediately.

Tomato Scrambled Eggs

Creamy and tangy, these scrambled eggs are a real delight for your taste buds.

Servings: 2

Ingredients:
2 tablespoons butter
4 eggs, beaten
2 tablespoons heavy cream
1 ripe tomato, diced
1 garlic clove, chopped
Salt, pepper to taste

Directions:
1. Whisk the eggs with the heavy cream, salt and pepper.
2. Heat the butter in a skillet. Stir in the tomato and garlic and sauté for 3 minutes. Then pour in the egg mixture and cook until the eggs are gently set, stirring all the time.
3. The final result should be set, but still creamy.
4. Serve immediately.

Sautéed Spinach and Poached Eggs

A delicate sauté and a delicious poached egg on top is all you need to start your day on a high note.

Servings: 2

Ingredients:
2 tablespoons olive oil
1 garlic clove, chopped
3 cups spinach, shredded
2 tablespoons lemon juice
2 eggs
2 slices toasted bread

Directions:
1. Heat the olive oil in a skillet and stir in the garlic and spinach. Sauté for 5-7 minutes, stirring occasionally. When done, adjust the taste with salt and pepper and add the lemon juice. Remove from heat.
2. In the meantime, bring a few cups of water to a boil. Stir in a pinch of salt.
3. When the water is boiling, crack open the eggs and drop them in the hot liquid. Cook briefly (not more than 2-3 minutes) then drain.
4. To serve, place the toasted bread on a plate. Top with the sautéed spinach and a poached egg.
5. Serve immediately.

Butter Eggs with Bacon and Spinach

Servings: 4

Ingredients:
4 tablespoons butter
4 eggs
4 slices bacon
4 cups spinach
Salt, pepper to taste

Directions:
1. Melt the butter in a skillet. Crack open the eggs and drop them in the melted butter.
2. Season with salt and pepper and fry the eggs to the desired doneness.
3. Place the eggs on a platter and put the bacon in the pan. Fry the bacon until crisp; then remove it from the pan as well.
4. Throw the spinach in the pan and sauté for a few minutes just until it begins to soften.
5. Spoon the spinach onto the same platter and serve right away.

Smoked Salmon Creamy Eggs

Smoked salmon is a bit fancy, but in this particular recipe it brings a rustic flavor. It's a delicious way to add a bit of kick to a standard egg recipe.

Servings: 2-4

Ingredients:
4 slices smoked salmon, sliced
6 eggs, beaten
4 tablespoons butter
1 tablespoon chopped dill
1 tablespoon chopped chives

Directions:
1. Melt the butter in a saucepan or skillet. Stir in the salmon and sauté for 1 minute. Then pour in the eggs.
2. Cook them on low to medium heat, stirring all the time until set, but creamy.
3. Stir in the dill and chives and serve immediately.

Potato Chip Frittata

A frittata is a mix between an omelet and a tart. It usually takes more than 10 minutes to make. However, this recipe offers a shortcut that will save you a lot of time when you're in a rush, and the dish will still taste like a traditional frittata.

Servings: 4-6

Ingredients:
6 eggs, beaten
1 green onion, chopped
Salt, pepper to taste
2 tablespoons olive oil
¼ cup plain yogurt
3 cups potato chips

Directions:
1. Mix the eggs with the green onion, yogurt, salt and pepper in a bowl. Then add the potato chips.

2. Heat the olive oil in a skillet. Pour in the egg mixture and cover with a lid.
3. Cook on low to medium heat for 5-10 minutes or until the top is set.
4. Serve the frittata right away.

Zucchini Frittata

Servings: 4-6

Ingredients:
1 zucchini, finely sliced
1 garlic clove, chopped
4 tablespoons olive oil
6 eggs, beaten
2 tablespoons chopped dill
2 tablespoons chopped parsley

Directions:
1. Heat the oil in a skillet and stir in the garlic and zucchini. Sauté for 2 minutes.
2. In the meantime, whisk the eggs with the dill and parsley.
3. Pour this mixture over the zucchini, then cover with a lid and cook on low to medium heat for 5-7 minutes.
4. If needed, flip the frittata over to finish cooking.
5. Serve the frittata warm.

Fresh Fruit with Yogurt Dip

Servings: 2-4

Ingredients:
1 ½ cups plain yogurt
1 teaspoon grated lemon zest
4 tablespoons honey
1 mint leaf, chopped
4 slices pineapple, cubed
1 ripe mango, cubed
1 orange, sliced

Directions:
1. Mix the yogurt with the honey, lemon zest and chopped mint in a small bowl.
2. Top fruit with the yogurt mix.
3. Refrigerate 1 hour before serving.

Sandwiches

Busy people often feel they can't afford a lunch break. 10 minutes will let you make a delicious and nutritious sandwich to tide you over.

6. Fried Egg and Arugula Sandwich

Serves: 2

Ingredients:
2 sandwich buns (choose your favorite bread)
2 eggs
2 tablespoons olive oil
2 tablespoons mayonnaise
2 tablespoons ketchup
1 cup arugula leaves
1 ripe tomato, sliced

Directions:
1. Heat the olive oil in a skillet. Crack open the eggs and drop them in the hot oil. Cook them until set.
2. Spread the mayonnaise on one or both halves of the buns. Place the eggs and top with arugula, tomato, mayonnaise and ketchup.
3. Serve immediately.

Cheddar Spread Sandwich

This Cheddar spread is incredibly good. Gooey, rich and creamy, your entire family will love it! However, it can only be served warm and fresh so make small batches that you can serve immediately.

Servings: 4

Ingredients:
1 ½ cups grated Cheddar cheese
½ cup cream cheese
1 teaspoon dry mustard
1 teaspoon Worcestershire sauce
1 drop hot sauce
4 bread buns
4 slices bacon, cooked

Directions:
1. Combine the cream cheese with the mustard, hot sauce, Worcestershire sauce and grated Cheddar in a saucepan and place on medium heat. Cook just until melted.
2. Cut the bread buns in half lengthwise and spread the cream cheese on each bun.
3. Top with bacon slices and serve immediately.

Monte Cristo Sandwich

This sandwich is a delight for your taste buds. The cranberry jam and smoky ham create an interesting taste contrast, making the sandwich irresistible.

Servings: 4

Ingredients:
8 slices whole wheat bread
¼ cup cranberry jam
4 thick slices smoked ham
1 tablespoon Dijon mustard

Directions:
1. Take 4 slices of bread and spread the cranberry jam over one slice for each sandwich.
2. Top with smoked ham and brush the opposite bread slice with mustard.
3. Place the remaining slices of bread on top to form the sandwiches.
4. Place the sandwiches in your sandwich maker and cook 2-3 minutes.
5. Serve them warm.

Apple and Cheddar Sandwich

Servings: 2

Ingredients:
1 green apple, cored and finely sliced
4 slices whole wheat bread
2 slices Cheddar cheese
1 pinch chili flakes
1 pinch nutmeg

Directions:
1. Place the apple and cheese on 2 slices of bread.
2. Sprinkle chili flakes and nutmeg over the cheese, then top with the remaining slices of bread to form the sandwiches.
3. Place the sandwiches in your sandwich maker and cook just 2-3 minutes until the cheese is melted.
4. Serve the sandwiches warm.

Roasted Bell Peppers Sandwich

Bell peppers have a sweet background taste and a smoky flavor that gets addictive. Now imagine them paired with feta cheese. It is heaven in a sandwich, I'm telling you!

Servings: 4

Ingredients:
8 slices whole wheat bread
4 roasted bell peppers
4 oz. feta cheese, crumbled
4 slices tomatoes
2 tablespoons olive oil

Directions:
1. Take 4 slices of bread. Drizzle them with olive oil. Then top with bell peppers, crumbled cheese and sliced tomatoes.
2. Top the sandwich with the remaining bread slices. Serve immediately.

Garlicky White Bean Sandwich

This white bean spread can be used in other dishes as well. Enjoy it in this rich and flavorful sandwich.

Servings: 4

Ingredients:
2 cups canned white beans, drained
2 garlic cloves, minced
2 tablespoons olive oil
2 tablespoons chopped parsley
4 roasted bell peppers
1 pickled cucumber, sliced
Salt, pepper to taste
8 slices white sandwich bread

Directions:
1. Mash the beans with a fork, then stir in the garlic, olive oil and parsley. Season with salt and pepper.
2. Spread the white bean mix on 4 slices of bread.
3. Place the bell peppers and cucumber on top, then top with the remaining slices of bread.
4. Serve right away.

Tuna Melt Panini

Servings: 4

Ingredients:
8 slices whole wheat bread or 4 bread buns
1 tin water canned tuna, drained
4 slices of a cheese of your choice
1 pinch freshly ground pepper

Directions:
1. Take 4 slices of bread and top them with tuna, cheese and a pinch of pepper, or use your favorite bread buns.
2. Place the remaining bread over the cheese to form the sandwiches.
3. Place the sandwiches in your sandwich maker and press them just until the cheese is melted.
4. Serve right away.

Lemony Caper and Tuna Sandwich

This sandwich combines the fresh taste of lemon with the saltiness of capers and the delicacy of tuna to create a sandwich that tastes truly heavenly.

Servings: 4

Ingredients:
4 slices whole wheat bread
1 tin water canned tuna
2 tablespoons lemon juice
1 teaspoon capers, chopped
1 green onion, finely chopped
Salt, pepper to taste

Directions:
1. Mix the tuna with the lemon juice, capers, green onion, salt and pepper to taste.
2. Spoon the tuna between two slices of bread and serve immediately.

Cucumber and Avocado Sandwich

The avocado replaces meat in this sandwich. Avocado is high in good fats and makes a healthy addition to your diet.

Servings: 4

Ingredients:
4 panini bread, cut in half lengthwise
1 ripe avocado, peeled and sliced
1 cucumber, sliced
1 cup arugula leaves
1/1 cup cherry tomatoes, sliced

Directions:
1. Fill each panini with avocado, cucumber, tomatoes and arugula.
2. Cook in the sandwich press for just a couple of minutes.
3. Serve right away.

Warm Fontina and Fig Sandwich

You will be impressed by how good this combination tastes.

Servings: 2

Ingredients:
2 bread buns
4 figs, sliced
1 cup arugula
2 thick slices Fontina cheese

Directions;
1. Top the bread bun half with figs, arugula and cheese then place the sandwiches in your sandwich maker.
2. Press and cook them for 2-3 minutes or until golden brown.
3. Serve the sandwiches immediately.

Salads

Salads are so versatile. You can basically make a different salad every day and never get bored.

7. Berry Lettuce Salad

The fruits in this salad add a tangy and fragrant taste that works great with the other ingredients.

Servings: 4-6

Ingredients:
1 head lettuce, shredded
2 cups arugula leaves
1 ½ cups mixed berries
½ cup crumbled Gorgonzola cheese
2 tablespoons balsamic vinegar
4 tablespoons lemon juice
4 tablespoons olive oil
Salt, pepper to taste

Directions:
1. Mix the lettuce with the arugula in a bowl.
2. Add the berries and gorgonzola and set aside.
3. To make the dressing, combine the lemon juice with the olive oil, balsamic vinegar and olive oil in a jar. Cover the jar with a lid and shake until well mixed.
4. Drizzle the dressing over the salad and mix gently. Season with salt and pepper to taste.
5. Serve the salad right away.

Cold Potato Salad

Servings: 2-4

Ingredients:
4 large potatoes, boiled
2 hard-boiled eggs, chopped
2 green onions, chopped
½ cup black olives, pitted
¼ cup green olives, pitted
2 tablespoons chopped parsley
Salt, pepper to taste
2 tablespoons lemon juice
2 tablespoons olive oil

Directions:
1. Combine all the ingredients in a large salad bowl.
2. Mix gently to evenly distribute the ingredients, then serve fresh.

Spinach and Strawberry Balsamico Salad

Servings: 2-4

Ingredients:
4 cups fresh spinach leaves
1 ½ cups fresh strawberries, sliced
4 tablespoons balsamic vinegar
2 tablespoons olive oil
Salt, pepper to taste

Directions:
1. Mix the strawberries with the vinegar and olive oil.
2. Place the spinach leaves in a salad bowl. Add the strawberries and balsamic sauce and mix gently.
3. Season with salt and pepper and serve the salad right away.

Plums and Mozzarella Salad

This is truly a surprising salad It is delicate, juicy and absolutely delicious.

Servings: 2-4

Ingredients:
½ head lettuce, shredded
8 plums, halved, pit removed
1 red onion, sliced
1 tablespoon lemon juice
1 tablespoon balsamic vinegar
2 tablespoons olive oil
½ teaspoon dried oregano
2 tablespoons chopped parsley
5 oz. mozzarella, shredded

Directions:
1. Combine the red onion, lemon juice, balsamic vinegar, olive oil, oregano and parsley in a bowl.
2. Stir in the plums and lettuce.
3. Top with mozzarella cheese and serve drizzled with the remaining marinade.

Tomato and Basil Salad

You won't see easier recipe than this one! All you have to do is slice tomatoes. The rest is easy, refreshing and delicious.

Servings: 2-4

Ingredients:
5 ripe tomatoes, sliced
4 basil leaves, shredded
5 oz. mozzarella cheese, crumbled

2 tablespoons olive oil
1 tablespoon balsamic vinegar
Salt, pepper to taste

Directions:
1. Mix the tomato slices, basil and mozzarella in a bowl. Add the vinegar and mix gently.
2. Stir in the olive oil and mix gently. Serve the salad fresh.

Watermelon and Blue Cheese Salad

Sweet and juicy watermelon pairs beautifully with fragrant and salty blue cheese. It's the perfect summer salad.

Servings: 2-4

Ingredients:
4 cups seedless watermelon cubes
4 oz. blue cheese, crumbled
4 tablespoons olive oil
1 pinch black pepper

Directions:
1. Combine the watermelon with the blue cheese in a salad bowl.
2. Season with freshly ground pepper and drizzle with olive oil, then serve.

Citrus Fennel Salad

Servings: 1-2

Ingredients:
1 fennel bulb, sliced
1 red onion, sliced
4 tablespoons olive oil
½ lemon, juiced
Salt, pepper to taste
½ cup black olives

Directions:
1. Mix the orange segments with the fennel bulbs and olives.
2. Drizzle with olive oil and lemon juice, then season with salt and pepper.
3. Mix gently and serve the salad fresh.

Watercress Lemon Salad

This salad is light and packed with nutrients.

Servings: 2-4

Ingredients:
4 cups watercress, rinsed
1 orange, cut into segments
½ lemon, juiced
1 teaspoon lemon zest
2 tablespoons olive oil
1 teaspoon balsamic vinegar
Salt, pepper to taste

Directions:
1. Mix the watercress with the orange segments in a bowl.
2. In a small jar, combine the lemon juice, lemon zest, olive oil, balsamic vinegar, salt and pepper. Cover with a lid and shake well until smooth.
3. Pour the dressing over the salad and mix gently.
4. Serve immediately.

Caprese Salad

This classic salad takes just a few minutes to make.

Servings: 2-4

Ingredients:
4 ripe tomatoes, sliced
4 oz. mozzarella cheese, sliced
4 basil leaves, shredded
3 tablespoons olive oil
Salt, pepper to taste

Directions:
1. Layer the tomatoes, mozzarella and basil on a platter.
2. Season with salt and pepper then drizzle with olive oil.
3. Serve the salad fresh.

Panzanella Salad

Panzanella is an Italian classic born of the need to use bread leftovers.

Servings: 2-4

Ingredients:
5 ripe tomatoes, cubed
1 cucumber, sliced
1 red onion, sliced
4 oz. feta cheese, cubes
4 slices whole wheat bread, cubed
4 tablespoons olive oil
2 tablespoons balsamic vinegar
Salt, pepper to taste

Directions:
1. Combine the tomatoes with the cucumber, onion, feta, olive oil and balsamic in a salad bowl.
2. Season with salt and pepper, then add the bread cubes and mix gently.
3. Serve the salad immediately.

Roast Beef Cabbage Salad

This is a filling and delicious salad that can replace dinner or lunch if you're a fan of light cooking.

Servings: 2-4

Ingredients:
1 small red cabbage, shredded
1 bunch parsley, chopped
1 red onion, sliced
5 oz. roasted beef, shredded
2 tablespoons balsamic vinegar
2 tablespoons lemon juice
2 tablespoons olive oil
Salt, pepper to taste

Directions:
1. Combine the cabbage with the parsley and red onion in a salad bowl. Stir in the balsamic vinegar, lemon juice and olive oil, then season with salt and pepper.
2. Add the roast beef and serve the salad immediately.

Bell Pepper and Quinoa Salad

Quinoa is considered a super grain because it has so many nutrients. It is easy to combine with vegetables.

Servings: 2-4

Ingredients:
4 roasted bell peppers, chopped
1 bunch cilantro, chopped
1 cucumber, sliced
1 red onion, sliced
2 cups cooked quinoa
½ lemon, juiced
2 tablespoons balsamic vinegar
2 tablespoons olive oil
Salt, pepper to taste

Directions:
1. Combine all the ingredients in a bowl.
2. Mix gently, then serve the salad right away.

Raw Zucchini and Sesame Salad

This salad has a nice crunch and a fresh taste, not to mention all the nutrients.

Servings: 2-4

Ingredients:
2 young zucchinis, sliced lengthwise
½ lemon, juiced
2 tablespoons olive oil
1 teaspoon sesame oil
¼ cup sesame seeds
Salt, pepper to taste

Directions:
1. Combine all the ingredients in a bowl.
2. Mix gently and serve the salad fresh as an entrée or side dish.

Rice and Sweet Corn Salad

Servings: 2-4

Ingredients:
2 cups cooked brown rice
1 red bell pepper, cored and diced
1 yellow bell pepper, cored and diced
2 tomatoes, sliced
1 red onion, sliced
¼ cup pitted black olives
1 cup sweet corn, drained
1 pickled cucumber, sliced
Salt, pepper to taste
2 tablespoons olive oil
2 tablespoons lemon juice

Directions:
1. Combine all the vegetables in a bowl, then stir in the rice.
2. Add salt and pepper to taste, then drizzle in the olive oil and lemon juice.
3. Mix gently and serve fresh.

Goat Cheese Salad

Salty and creamy goat cheese deserves a dish that makes it shine and this salad certainly does.

Servings: 2-4

Ingredients:
1 head lettuce, shredded
6 figs, quartered
4 purple basil leaves, shredded

1 teaspoon honey
1 teaspoon Dijon mustard
2 tablespoons olive oil
2 tablespoons lemon juice
Salt, pepper to taste
4 oz. goat cheese, crumbled

Directions:
1. Mix the shredded lettuce with the figs and basil in a salad bowl.
2. In a small bowl, combine the honey, mustard, olive oil, lemon juice, salt and pepper and mix well.
3. Pour the dressing over the salad and mix gently.
4. Serve the salad fresh, topped with the goat cheese.

Main Dishes

This chapter includes 25 recipes of main dishes that despite the short cooking time taste amazing — and shine with simplicity of flavors.

8. Cheese Tortellini with Sun-Dried Tomatoes

Servings: 2-4

Ingredients:
1 pound pre-cooked cheese tortellini
2 tablespoons olive oil
2 tablespoons butter
2 cups fresh spinach
¼ cup sun-dried tomatoes, chopped
Salt, pepper to taste

Directions:
1. Mix the butter and olive oil in a skillet.
2. Stir in the spinach, tomatoes and tortellini and cook on low to medium heat for 7-10 minutes.
3. Season with salt and pepper if needed and serve immediately.

Garlic and Tomato Pasta

Servings: 2-4

Ingredients:
6 oz. pasta of your choice
3 ripe tomatoes, diced
3 garlic cloves, chopped
2 tablespoons olive oil
½ teaspoon dried basil
Salt, pepper to taste

½ cup grated Parmesan

Directions:
1. Cook the pasta in a large pot of salty water. Drain and set aside.
2. While the pasta is cooking, heat the olive oil in a skillet. Stir in the garlic and sauté for 1 minute, then add the tomatoes and basil and cook for 6-7 minutes on low heat.
3. Stir in the pasta and mix gently.
4. Serve fresh and warm. Top with Parmesan.

Bok Choy Stir Fry with Peanuts

Servings: 2-4

Ingredients:
2 bok choy, shredded
2 garlic cloves
1 teaspoon grated ginger
2 tablespoons vegetable oil
½ teaspoon sesame oil
1 tablespoon soy sauce
½ cup peanuts

Directions:
1. Heat the oil in a wok. Stir in the garlic and ginger and sauté 30 seconds. Then add the bok choy.
2. Sauté for 5 minutes, then stir in the sesame oil, soy sauce and peanuts.
3. Cook 2 more minutes and serve.

Bacon and Avocado Scrambled Egg

Scrambled eggs aren't just for breakfast. This recipe is filling and rich and can be served for lunch or dinner when you're not sure what to whip up in hurry.

Servings: 2-4

Ingredients:
5 eggs, beaten
1 ripe avocado, peeled and cubed
4 bacon slices, chopped
1 pinch chili flakes

Directions:
1. Heat a skillet over medium flame. Add the bacon and fry it until crisp, then stir in the avocado.
2. Pour in the eggs and chili flakes and mix until set.
3. Serve warm.

Sautéed Tilapia with Tomato Sauce

Servings: 4

Ingredients:
4 tilapia fillets
Salt, pepper to taste
3 tablespoons olive oil
1 cup cherry tomatoes, halved

Directions:
1. Heat the olive oil in a skillet.
2. Season the tilapia with salt and pepper and place in the hot oil.
3. Cook the fillets 2-3 minutes on each side, depending on the thickness of the fish. Remove from the pan.
4. Throw the tomatoes in the pan and sauté them for 2-3 minutes. They don't have to cook all the way through.
5. Serve.

Tomato Sauce Spaghetti

This tomato sauce is very easy and quick to make and it can be served with spaghetti or other pasta. It can also be frozen for later.

Servings: 2-4

Ingredients:
1 can diced tomatoes
1 garlic clove, chopped
2 tablespoons olive oil
½ teaspoon dried basil
½ teaspoon dried oregano
Salt, pepper to taste
6 oz. spaghetti

Directions:
1. Puree the tomatoes in a blender, then combine the puree with the garlic, olive oil, basil and oregano in a saucepan. Cook for 5-10 minutes until it begins to thicken.

2. While the sauce is simmering, cook the pasta in a large pot of salty water just until al dente.
3. Drain the spaghetti and mix with the sauce.
4. Serve right away.

Spicy Pecorino Spaghetti

The key for this recipe is a good quality olive oil and the best Pecorino you can afford.

Servings: 2-4

Ingredients:
8 oz. spaghetti
1 garlic clove, chopped
4 tablespoons extra virgin olive oil
1 pinch chili flakes
1 cup grated Pecorino

Directions:
1. Cook the pasta in a large pot of salty water.
2. While the pasta is cooking, heat the olive oil in a skillet. Stir in the garlic and sauté 30 seconds.
3. Drain the pasta and set aside.
4. Remove the oil and garlic from heat and add the pasta and chili flakes. Mix to coat the spaghetti.
5. Transfer onto serving plates and top with plenty of grated Pecorino.
6. Serve immediately.

Lemon and Cilantro Roasted Salmon

Servings: 4

Ingredients:
4 salmon fillets
1 lemon, juiced
2 tablespoons olive oil
2 tablespoons chopped cilantro
Salt, pepper to taste

Directions:
1. Mix the lime juice, olive oil and cilantro in a bowl. Add salt and pepper to taste.
2. Place the salmon fillets on a baking tray. Top with the cilantro mixture and roast at 400 °F for 7-8 minutes.
3. Serve the fish warm with your favorite side dish.

Shrimp and Spring Onion Stir Fry

Servings: 2-4

Ingredients:
3 tablespoons vegetable oil
2 pounds shrimps, peeled and deveined
2 green onions, chopped
½ lime, juiced
Salt, pepper to taste

Directions:
1. Heat the oil in a wok. Stir in the shrimp and cook them 5-7 minutes just until they turn pink.
2. Add the spring onions and lime juice, as well as salt and pepper to taste. Cook 1 more minute.
3. Serve the stir fry immediately.

Pan Fried Sole

Servings: 4

Ingredients:
4 sole fillets
½ lemon, sliced
4 tablespoons olive oil
1 garlic clove, crushed
Salt, pepper to taste

Directions:
1. Season the fish with salt and pepper.
2. Heat the olive oil in a skillet. Add the garlic and lemon and cook for 2 minutes, just until they release their flavor.
3. Remove the garlic and lemon and add the sole fillets. Fry them 2-3 minutes on each side, depending on thickness, over medium heat.
4. Serve the fish with your favorite side dish.

White Wine Shrimps

Servings: 2-4

Ingredients:
2 pounds fresh shrimp, peeled and deveined
1 garlic clove, chopped
1 teaspoon dried oregano
3 tablespoons olive oil
¼ cup white wine
Salt, pepper to taste

Directions:
1. Heat the oil in a skillet and stir in the garlic and oregano. Sauté 30 seconds then add the shrimp.
2. Cook them for 2 minutes then pour in the white wine.
3. Season with salt and pepper and cook on high heat for 3-4 more minutes (or until the shrimp have just turned pink).
4. Serve the shrimp with your favorite side dish.

Quick Flatbread Pizza

Although traditionally pizza is made in more than 10 minutes, this recipe uses flatbread as a base and is made in a skillet.

Servings: 2

Ingredients:
2 flat breads
1 ripe tomato, sliced
¼ cup pitted black olives, chopped
4 oz. mozzarella, shredded
2 tablespoons olive oil

Directions:
1. Brush the flatbread with olive oil. Top them with tomato slices, black olives and mozzarella.
2. Place flatbread(s) in a skillet. Cover with a lid and cook on high heat for 5-7 minutes.
3. Serve immediately.

Quick Fried Rice

Servings: 2-4

Ingredients:
3 cups cooked long grain rice
2 eggs
½ teaspoon sesame oil
2 tablespoons olive oil
½ cup green peas
½ cup canned sweet corn, drained
1 tablespoon soy sauce

Directions:
1. Heat the olive oil in a skillet and stir in the green peas and corn.
2. Sauté 2 minutes, then add the rice.
3. Whisk the eggs with the soy sauce and sesame oil and pour it over the rice.
4. Cook for a few minutes, stirring often, until the eggs are set.

5. Serve the rice right away.

Lettuce Wraps

Servings: 4

Ingredients:
1 ripe avocado, peeled and sliced
2 ripe tomatoes, sliced
1 cucumber, sliced
1 red onion, sliced
4 oz. feta cheese, cubed
¼ cup mayonnaise
¼ cup ketchup
4 lettuce leaves

Directions:
1. Place the lettuce leaves on a clean working surface and top each with avocado, tomatoes, cucumber, red onion and feta.
2. Drizzle with mayonnaise and ketchup; then wrap each leaf as tightly as possible.
3. Serve.

Chicken Wraps

Servings: 4

Ingredients:
4 flour tortillas
2 cooked chicken breasts, shredded
2 red bell peppers, cored and sliced
2 cups baby spinach leaves
½ cup plain yogurt
1 pinch chili flakes
¼ cup ketchup

Directions:
1. Lay the tortillas on clean a working surface.
2. Place the chicken, peppers, spinach, yogurt and ketchup in the center of each tortilla then wrap them tight.
3. Sprinkle with chili flakes and serve.

Cucumber and Yogurt Cold Soup

This cold soup is rich and creamy and so refreshing.

Servings: 2-4

Ingredients:
2 cucumbers
2 cups Greek style yogurt
6 ice cubes
Salt, pepper to taste
2 tablespoons chopped dill
2 tablespoons olive oil

Directions:
1. Mix the cucumber with the yogurt, ice cubes, salt and pepper in a blender and pulse until smooth.
2. Fold in the chopped dill, then pour in serving bowls.
3. Drizzle with olive oil and serve chilled.

Gazpacho

Gazpacho is best made and served right away.

Servings: 4-6

Ingredients:
4 ripe tomatoes, peeled and cubed
1 cucumber, sliced
1 shallot, sliced
2 red bell peppers, cored and sliced

1 garlic clove, peeled
1 cup water
Salt, pepper to taste
2 tablespoons olive oil
2 tablespoons chopped parsley for serving
Ice cubes for serving

Directions:
1. Mix all the ingredients in a blender.
2. Pulse until smooth; then pour in serving bowls.
3. Top with chopped parsley and serve with ice cubes.

Angel Hair Pasta with Smoked Trout

Servings: 2-4

Ingredients:
10 oz. angel hair pasta
2 tablespoons olive oil
2 garlic cloves, chopped
1 teaspoon lemon zest
2 tablespoons lemon juice
2 smoked trout fillets, shredded
1 pinch chili flakes
Salt, pepper to taste

Directions:
1. Cook the angel hair pasta until al dente.
2. While the pasta cooks, heat the olive oil in a skillet and stir in the garlic, lemon zest, lemon juice, chili flakes and trout.
3. Sauté for 5-10 minutes. As the ingredients sauté, drain the pasta and set it aside.
4. When the sauce is cooked, stir in the pasta.
5. Season with salt and pepper and serve warm.

Baked Eggs with Fresh Herbs

Servings: 4

Ingredients:
4 eggs
2 tablespoons chopped chives
1 tablespoon chopped parsley
4 tablespoons olive oil
Salt, pepper to taste

Directions:
1. Pour the olive oil in 4 small microwave safe baking cups.
2. Crack open the eggs and place them in each cup.
3. Sprinkle with salt and freshly ground pepper, and top them with chopped chives and parsley.
4. Cook the eggs in the microwave for 1-2 minutes on high.
5. Serve.

Cajun Mushrooms

Servings: 2-4

Ingredients:
2 tablespoons olive oil
1 pound mushrooms, sliced
1 pinch chili flakes
2 garlic cloves, chopped
1 teaspoon dried oregano
¼ teaspoon turmeric powder
½ teaspoon Cajun seasoning
Salt, pepper to taste

Directions:
1. Heat the olive oil in a skillet.
2. Stir in the garlic and mushrooms and sauté for 6-8 minutes

on high heat.
3. Add the chili flakes, oregano, Cajun seasoning and turmeric and serve the mushrooms warm.

Spinach and Cheddar Tortilla Melts

Servings: 4

Ingredients:
4 flour tortillas
2 cups grated Cheddar cheese
2 cups baby spinach leaves
1 pinch chili flakes
1 pinch nutmeg

Directions:
1. Mix the cheese, spinach, chili flakes and nutmeg in a bowl.
2. Coat the tortillas with the cheese mixture; add more cheese before adding the top tortilla, if desired.
3. Place the tortillas in a sandwich press and cook until the cheese melts.
4. Cut into triangles or quarters with a pizza cutter and serve.

Gooey Cheese Croissants

Cheddar and a touch of blue cheese turn some simple croissants into the most delicious meal.

Servings: 4

Ingredients:
4 croissants, cut in half lengthwise
1 ½ cups grated Cheddar cheese
2 oz. blue cheese, crumbled
½ cup cherry tomatoes, halved

Directions:
1. Top each croissant half with tomatoes, grated Cheddar and blue cheese. Add the second half to make a delicious, unique sandwich.
2. Place the croissants under the broiler for 5-7 minutes.
3. Serve warm.

Cheese and Sausage Roll

Servings: 4

Ingredients:
4 long bread rolls, cut lengthwise
4 smoked sausages
4 tablespoons ketchup
2 tablespoons mustard
1 cup grated cheese

Directions:
1. Top each bread roll half with one sausage, ketchup, mustard and cheese. Add the top half.
2. Place the rolls under the broiler for 5-7 minutes until the cheese is melted.
3. Serve the rolls right away.

Cheese Stuffed Mushrooms

These earthy, delicate stuffed mushrooms are delicious served either warm or chilled.

Servings: 4

Ingredients:
4 large mushrooms
2 basil leaves, shredded

2 ripe tomatoes, diced
1 pinch chili flakes
1 cup shredded cheese of your choice
Salt, pepper to taste

Directions:
1. Mix all the ingredients except the mushrooms in a bowl. Season with salt and pepper to taste.
2. Spoon the filling into each mushroom and place the mushrooms under the broiler.
3. Cook for 5-7 minutes on high heat or until the cheese is melted.
4. Serve them warm or chilled.

Gnocchi with Three Cheese Sauce

Pre-cooked gnocchi are a good shortcut for a quick meal. They shine with this three-cheese sauce.

Servings: 2-4

Ingredients:
1 cup heavy cream
½ cup grated Cheddar cheese
¼ cup grated Parmesan cheese
½ cup shredded mozzarella
1 pinch nutmeg
1 pound gnocchi

Directions:
1. Mix the heavy cream, Cheddar cheese, Parmesan, mozzarella and nutmeg in a saucepan. Cook on low heat just until melted.
2. Stir in the gnocchi and cook 2-3 more minutes.
3. Serve warm.

Side Dishes

These side dishes are all delicious and healthy, loaded with fresh ingredients and intense flavors.

9. Lemon Zucchini Sauté

Servings: 2-4

Ingredients:
2 young zucchini, sliced
2 tablespoons olive oil
1 garlic clove, chopped
2 tablespoons lemon juice
½ cup grated Parmesan cheese
Salt, pepper to taste

Directions:
1. Heat the olive oil in a skillet. Add the garlic and sauté for 30 seconds.
2. Add the zucchini slices and lemon juice and cook for 5-7 minutes.
3. Season with salt and pepper and spoon on serving platters. Top with grated Parmesan just before serving.

Spicy Snap Peas

Servings: 2-4

Ingredients:
1 ½ pounds snap peas
4 tablespoons olive oil
¼ lemon, juice
1 red pepper, sliced
Salt, pepper to taste
1 green onion, sliced

Directions:
1. Heat the olive oil in a skillet. Stir in the snap peas and cook them for 2-4 minutes on high heat, stirring often.
2. Stir in the lemon juice, red pepper, salt, pepper and green onion and cook 4-5 more minutes.
3. Serve warm.

Garlicky Sautéed Spinach with Sweet Corn

Servings: 2-3

Ingredients:
1 ½ pounds baby spinach
2 garlic cloves, chopped
4 tablespoons olive oil
1 pinch chili flakes
1 pinch nutmeg
Salt, pepper to taste
2 tablespoons lemon juice
½ cup sweet corn, drained

Directions:
1. Heat the olive oil in a skillet and stir in the garlic. Sauté for 30 seconds then add the spinach, chili flakes and nutmeg.
2. Season with salt and pepper and cook for 5-7 minutes on high heat, stirring often.
3. When done, sprinkle with lemon juice and serve right away.

Yogurt and Blueberry Trifle

4. Microwave Chocolate Cake   111
5.
6. Ricotta and Berry Dessert   112
7.
8. Meringue and Strawberry Dessert 114
9.
10.
11. Melba Grilled Peaches   116
12. Yogurt with Pistachio and Strawberry Bowls   117
13. Caramelized Pears   118
14. Fresh Pears with Pecan Topping   119
15. Grilled Pineapple and Ginger Sauce   120
16. Watermelon and Raspberry Salad 122
17. Spiced Poached Apricots   123
18. Banana Ice Cream   124
19. *Beverages*   *125*
20. Spiced Hot Cocoa   125
21. Watermelon Lemonade 127
22. Spinach Smoothie   128
23. Detox Juice   130
24. Chilled Fruit Shake 131
25. Margarita Shake   133
26. **Conclusion**   **134**
27.

Crispy Couscous

Servings: 2-4

Ingredients:
4 cups cooked couscous
1 ripe tomato, diced
1 small cucumber, chopped
¼ cup dried apricots, chopped
½ cup roasted hazelnuts, chopped
2 tablespoons lemon juice
2 tablespoons balsamic vinegar
Salt, pepper to taste

Directions:
1. Combine the cooked couscous with the tomato, cucumber, apricots and hazelnuts in a bowl.
2. Stir in the lemon juice and balsamic vinegar, then season with salt and pepper to taste.
3. Mix gently and serve.

Bacon Green Peas

Either fresh or frozen, green peas require very little cooking time. If overcooked, they become mushy.

Servings: 2-4

Ingredients:
4 bacon slices, chopped
3 cups green peas
2 mint leaves, chopped
½ teaspoon dried oregano
Salt, pepper to taste

Directions:
1. Heat a skillet over medium flame and stir in the bacon.
2. Cook until crisp then add the green peas, mint, oregano, salt and pepper.
3. Sauté for 4-5 minutes and serve.

Lemony Poached Asparagus

Servings: 2-4

Ingredients:
2 bunches green asparagus, trimmed
Salt, pepper to taste
2 tablespoons olive oil
2 tablespoons lemon juice
1 teaspoon lemon zest
4 prosciutto slices

Directions:
1. Bring a large pot of water to a boil. Add a pinch of salt and throw in the asparagus. Cook for 5 minutes on high heat, then drain and place into a bowl.
2. Stir in the olive oil, lemon juice and lemon zest, then season with salt and pepper.
3. Serve the asparagus with prosciutto slices.

Chickpea Curry

Canned chickpeas are one of the best shortcuts in the kitchen. Cooking fresh chickpeas takes a long time, but this way you can enjoy chickpeas right away. Mix them with tomatoes and curry and you've got yourself a delicious and rich side dish.

Servings: 2-4

Ingredients:
1 tin canned chickpeas, drained
1 cup canned diced tomatoes
1 teaspoon curry paste
2 garlic cloves, chopped
3 tablespoons olive oil
Salt, pepper to taste

Directions:
1. Heat the olive oil in a skillet and stir in the garlic. Sauté for 30 seconds.
2. Add the chickpeas, tomatoes and curry paste, then season with salt and pepper.
3. Cook the chickpeas on high heat for about 8 minutes, then serve warm.

Sautéed Tomatoes

Servings: 2-4

Ingredients:
4 large ripe tomatoes, sliced
4 tablespoons olive oil
2 garlic cloves, chopped
½ teaspoon dried oregano
½ teaspoon dried basil
Salt, pepper to taste

Directions:
1. Heat the olive oil in a large skillet and stir in the garlic. Sauté 30 seconds then add the tomato slices.
2. Cook for 5-7 minutes, then add the rest of the ingredients.
3. Season with salt and freshly ground pepper and serve warm.

Avocado and Tomato Salsa

Servings: 2-4

Ingredients:
1 ripe avocado, peeled and diced
3 ripe tomatoes, diced
1 shallot, finely chopped
2 tablespoons chopped cilantro
2 tablespoons chopped parsley
Salt, pepper to taste

Directions:
1. Combine all the ingredients in a bowl and mix gently.
2. Serve the salsa right away.

Cheddar Grits

Servings: 2-4

Ingredients:
4 cups hot water
1 cup uncooked quick cooking grits
1 ½ grated Cheddar cheese
2 tablespoons butter
¼ teaspoon garlic powder
1 teaspoon dried thyme
1 pinch nutmeg
1 pinch black pepper

Directions:
1. Combine the grits and the water in a saucepan and cook over high heat for 5-7 minutes, or until most of the liquid has been absorbed.
2. Remove from heat and stir in the cheese, butter, garlic powder, thyme, nutmeg and black pepper.
3. Briefly return the grits to low heat, mix well and serve.

Caramelized Red Onions

Servings: 1-2

Ingredients:
2 large red onions, sliced
3 tablespoons olive oil
1 teaspoon honey
1 tablespoon balsamic vinegar
1 pinch dried thyme
Salt, pepper to taste

Directions:
1. Heat the oil in a skillet and stir in the onions.
2. Cook on high heat for a few minutes until the liquid from the onions begins to evaporate.
3. Add the honey, thyme, salt and pepper and keep cooking on high heat until the onions are golden brown.
4. When done, remove from heat and stir in the vinegar.
5. Serve right away.

Cheesy Creamed Corn

Servings: 2-4

Ingredients:
2 cups heavy cream
1 cup grated Cheddar cheese
1 tablespoon flour
3 cups canned corn, drained and rinsed
½ teaspoon garlic powder
½ teaspoon dried rosemary

Salt, pepper to taste

Directions:
1. Combine all the ingredients in a heavy saucepan.
2. Place over medium to high heat and cook, stirring all the time until thick and creamy.
3. Remove from heat and season with salt and pepper.
4. Serve immediately.

Cheese Cauliflower Sauté

Servings: 2-4

Ingredients:
1 head cauliflower, cut into florets
3 tablespoons butter
½ teaspoon garlic powder
2 tablespoons chopped parsley
1 pinch nutmeg
1 cup grated Cheddar cheese

Directions:
1. Melt the butter in a large skillet.
2. Stir in the cauliflower florets and sauté them for about 5 minutes on high heat.
3. Stir in the garlic powder, parsley and nutmeg and cook 2 more minutes then remove from heat and top with grated cheese.
4. Serve right away.

10. Coconut Rice

Servings: 2-4

Ingredients:
2 cups uncooked instant white rice
1 can coconut milk
¼ cup coconut flakes
1 tablespoon butter
Salt, pepper to taste
1 pinch chili flakes

Directions:
1. Mix the white rice with the coconut milk and coconut flakes and cook on high heat for 5-10 minutes until all the liquid has been absorbed.
2. Add a tablespoon of butter, plus salt and pepper to taste, a pinch of chili flakes, and mix well.
3. Serve the rice warm.

Microwave Risotto

Risotto usually takes time, but this is a shortcut recipe, one that can be made in a microwave.

Servings: 2-4

Ingredients:
1 ½ cups instant white rice
3 cups chicken stock
1 shallot, chopped

2 tablespoons olive oil
Salt, pepper to taste
½ cup grated Parmesan cheese
1 cup green peas

Directions:
1. Combine the rice with the stock, shallot and olive oil in a microwave safe bowl.
2. Cook for 2 minutes on high, then remove from the microwave and mix with a fork.
3. Add salt and pepper, as well as the green peas and cook 5 more minutes.
4. Remove from the microwave and stir in the grated cheese.
5. Serve the risotto warm.

Dessert

Although most of the recipes in this section include fresh fruit, there's also a recipe for decadent chocolate cake and the simplest ice cream ever. Read on!

11. Minty Fruit Salad

Servings: 2-4

Ingredients:
2 oranges, cut into segments
1 grapefruits, cut into segments
1 cup fresh strawberries, quartered
1 banana, sliced
1 cup red grapes, halved
1 tablespoon lemon juice
2 tablespoons honey
4 mint leaves, chopped

Directions:
1. Combine the fruit with the lemon juice and mint leaves in a bowl.
2. Drizzle with honey and mix gently.
3. Serve the salad immediately.

Fruit and Mint Kebabs

Kids will adore these colorful and fun kebabs. Pair them with yogurt sauce and the dessert is complete.

Servings: 2-4

Ingredients:
1 cup red grapes
1 cup strawberries
1 cup melon cubes
2 apples, cored and cubed
2 tablespoons lemon juice
½ cup Greek style yogurt
1 teaspoon lemon zest
2 tablespoons honey
½ teaspoon vanilla extract
2-4 wooden skewers

Directions:
1. Place the fruit on wooden skewers in the order desired and set aside.
2. For the sauce, mix the yogurt with the lemon zest, honey and vanilla.
3. To serve, dip the kebabs into the yogurt sauce.

Orange and Yogurt Salad

Servings: 2

Ingredients:
1 cup plain yogurt
2 oranges, cut into segments
1 tablespoon chia seeds
1 tablespoon honey

Directions:
1. Mix the yogurt with the chia seeds and honey, then gently fold in the orange segments.
2. Serve the salad immediately.

Yogurt and Blueberry Trifle

Servings: 2

Ingredients:
1 cup Greek style yogurt
1 cup blueberries
1 cup crushed sugar cookies
½ cup dark chocolate chips

Directions:

1. Layer the crushed cookies, yogurt, peaches and chocolate chips in 2 serving glasses.
2. Serve the trifle immediately or refrigerate it.

Microwave Chocolate Cake

Servings: 1

Ingredients:
2 tablespoons flour
3 tablespoons sugar
2 tablespoons cocoa powder
1 egg
4 tablespoons milk
4 tablespoons vegetable oil
½ teaspoon vanilla extract

Directions:
1. Combine the ingredients in a microwave safe mug and mix well.
2. Place the mug in the microwave and bake the cake at high power for 1 ½ minutes. (Don't bake it more or it will dry out.)
3. Serve hot.

Ricotta and Berry Dessert

Ricotta is a fresh and mild cheese that works great in desserts, even recipes that require no baking, like this one. A few berries is all you need for a luscious dessert.

Servings: 2

Ingredients:
1 ½ cups fresh ricotta cheese
½ teaspoon vanilla extract

4 tablespoons honey
½ teaspoon lemon zest
1 cup fresh berries

Directions:
1. Mix the ricotta with the vanilla, honey and lemon zest, then spoon the mixture into two serving bowls.
2. Top with fresh berries and serve right away.

Meringue and Strawberry Dessert

You will love fragrant and fluffy dessert.

Servings: 2

Ingredients:
1 cup fresh strawberries, quartered
1 cup whipped cream
3 oz. of meringue, crushed
½ cup chocolate sauce

Directions:
1. Mix the strawberries with the whipped cream and crushed meringue.
2. Transfer into two serving bowls and top with chocolate sauce or extra whipped cream.
3. Serve.

Melba Grilled Peaches

Smoky and tender, these grilled peaches will surprise you.

Servings: 2

Ingredients:
4 ripe peaches, halved
2 tablespoons honey
2 scoops raspberry ice cream

Directions:
1. Brush the peaches with the honey and place them on a hot grill pan.
2. Cook until lightly browned, then place on a platter.
3. Top with vanilla ice cream and serve right away.

Yogurt with Pistachio and Strawberry Bowls

Fresh and healthy, this dessert is perfect for the entire family. And very easy to make. Invite the kids to help!

Servings: 2

Ingredients:
1 ½ cups Greek style yogurt
2 tablespoons honey
1 teaspoon lemon juice
½ cup crushed pistachios
1 cup fresh strawberries, halved
½ cup crushed sugar cookies

Directions:
1. Mix the yogurt with the honey, lemon juice and pistachios.
2. Spoon the yogurt into two serving bowls and top with fresh strawberries.
3. Sprinkle with crushed cookies and serve.

12. Caramelized Pears

Servings: 4

Ingredients:
4 ripe pears, peeled and halved
4 tablespoons brown sugar
¼ cup fresh orange juice
2 tablespoons butter
2 tablespoons dark rum

Directions:
1. Melt the sugar in a skillet on high heat. Add the butter, orange juice and rum, then place the pears in the pan.
2. Cook them for 5-7 minutes on high heat, flipping them over a few times to evenly coat them in sauce.
3. Serve them warm or chilled, plain or with ice cream.

13. Fresh Pears with Pecan Topping

Servings: 4

Ingredients:
2 ripe pears, halved and cored
½ cup pecans, crushed
4 tablespoons maple syrup
¼ teaspoon cinnamon powder
½ teaspoon orange zest
2 tablespoons rolled oats

Directions:
1. In a small bowl, mix the pecans, maple syrup, cinnamon, orange zest and oats.
2. Place the halved pears on a serving platter and top them with the pecan mixture.
3. Serve.

Grilled Pineapple and Ginger Sauce

Pineapple has a high sugar content, which means that it will caramelize beautifully on the grill. This delicious dessert can be served with the fragrant ginger sauce recipe listed here, or with ice cream if you prefer.

Servings: 2

Ingredients:
4 slices fresh pineapple
½ cup plain yogurt
2 tablespoons maple syrup
1 tablespoon grated ginger
1 pinch nutmeg
1 pinch cinnamon

Directions:
1. Heat a grill pan over medium flame.
2. Place the pineapple on the grill and cook on both sides until lightly browned.
3. In the meantime, mix the yogurt with the maple syrup, ginger, nutmeg and cinnamon.
4. Remove the pineapple from the pan. Serve on plates and top the pineapple with the yogurt sauce or your favorite ice cream.

Watermelon and Raspberry Salad

Servings: 2-4

Ingredients:
3 cups seedless watermelon cubes
1 ½ cups fresh raspberry
1 mint leaf, chopped
¼ lemon, juiced
1 tablespoon brown sugar

Directions:
1. Combine all the ingredients in a bowl.
2. Mix gently and serve.

14. Spiced Poached Apricots

Servings: 2-4

Ingredients
1 ½ pounds fresh apricots, halved and pitted
2 cups water
2 orange peels
½ lemon, juiced
4 tablespoons brown sugar
1 star anise

Directions:
1. Combine all the ingredients in a saucepan and cook for 6-8 minutes, just until the apricots are slightly tender.
2. Serve the apricots warm or chilled.

Banana Ice Cream

Servings: 2

Ingredients:
4 ripe bananas, frozen

Directions:
1. Place the bananas in your blender.
2. Pulse until creamy and smooth.
3. Serve right away or freeze in an airtight container.
4. Add your favorite toppings, if desired.

Beverages

The drinks in this chapter will brighten up your day. They are simple to make and amazingly delicious.

15. Spiced Hot Cocoa

There is nothing better than a cup of hot cocoa during the cold season. And this spiced hot cocoa is a real delight.

Servings: 2-4
Ingredients:
3 cups milk

1 cup heavy cream
½ cup cocoa powder
¼ cup brown sugar
¼ teaspoon cinnamon powder
1 pinch ground ginger
1 pinch nutmeg
1 star anise
½ teaspoon vanilla extract

Directions:
1. Mix all the ingredients in a saucepan and bring to a boil.
2. Lower the heat and simmer for 2-4 minutes; then pour the cocoa into cups and serve.

16. Watermelon Lemonade

Servings: 4-6

Ingredients:
1 cup seedless watermelon cubes
3 lemons, juiced
1 cup sugar
2 cups water
2 cups sparkling water
2 cups ice cubes

Directions:
1. Slightly crush the watermelon.
2. Mix the watermelon with the lemon juice and sugar in a glass jar.
3. Pour in the ice cubes, water and sparkling water and mix gently.
4. Serve.

Spinach Smoothie

This is one spinach smoothie that tastes great.

Servings: 4

Ingredients:
2 cups baby spinach
½ cup watermelon cubes
1 cup fresh strawberries
½ cup plain yogurt

2 cups almond milk
2 tablespoons honey

Directions:
1. Place all the ingredients in a blender.
2. Pulse until smooth and creamy.
3. Pour the smoothie in glasses of your choice and serve.

Detox Juice

Servings: 2-4

Ingredients:
2 cups spinach
4 kale leaves
2 green apples
1 cup fresh blueberries
½ -inch piece of ginger
1 grapefruit

Directions:
1. In a quality juicer, juice each of the ingredients.
2. Mix gently and serve immediately.

Chilled Fruit Shake

Servings: 2-4

Ingredients:
1 ripe banana
½ cup fresh strawberries
½ cup fresh blueberries
4 scoops vanilla ice cream
2 cups low fat milk
2 tablespoons honey

Directions:
1. Mix all the ingredients in a blender.
2. Pulse until well blended and smooth.
3. Pour into glasses of your choice and serve.

Margarita Shake

This beverage is for grown-ups. It's creamy and delicious without having too much alcohol.

Servings: 2-4

Ingredients:
4 scoops vanilla ice cream
2 scoops lemon sorbet
2 scoops lime sorbet
½ cup crushed ice
1 cup chilled soda water
¼ cup tequila

Directions:
1. Combine all the ingredients in a blender and pulse briefly just to mix them up.
2. Pour in glasses and serve right away.

Conclusion

Breakfast, main dishes, side dishes, desserts and even drink recipes, all in one place – easy to reach and easy to follow, all designed to meet your needs. I hope you've enjoyed this book.

Happy and healthy eating!

www.ingramcontent.com/pod-product-compliance
Lightning Source LLC
LaVergne TN
LVHW020419070526
838199LV00055B/3661